D1709454

WHAT ON EARTH?
Climate Change Explained

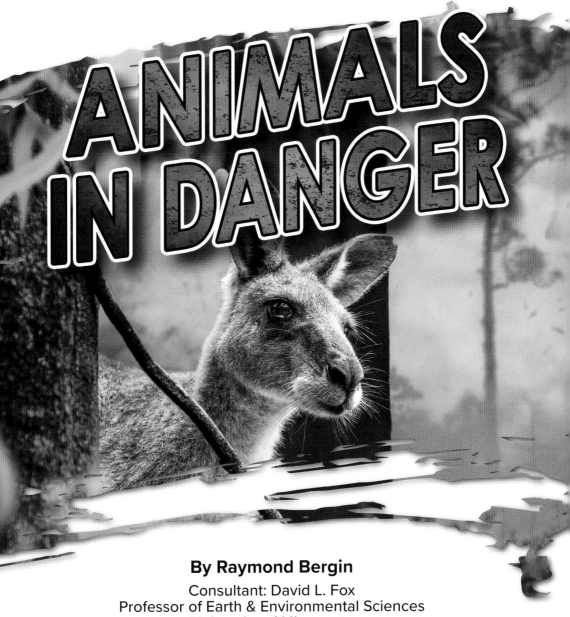

ANIMALS IN DANGER

By Raymond Bergin

Consultant: David L. Fox
Professor of Earth & Environmental Sciences
University of Minnesota

BEARPORT
PUBLISHING

Minneapolis, Minnesota

Credits

Cover and title page, © lindsay_imagery/iStockphoto, © Pgiam/iStockphoto;
4–5, © Daniel A. Leifheit/Getty; 6–7, © NASA/Wikimedia; 8–9, © SeppFriedhuber/
iStockphoto; 10–11, © Brett Monroe Garner/Getty; 12–13, © Fernando Frazao/iStockphoto;
14–15, © WLDavies/iStockphoto; 17, © Skip Moody /Alamy; 18–19, © ELENAPHOTOS/
iStockphoto; 20–21, © Volodymyr Burdiak/Shutterstock; 22–23, © Boy_Anupong/Getty,
© nityananda mukherjee/iStockphoto; 25, © WildMedia/Shutterstock; 26–27, © Image
Source/Alamy; 28, © guenterguni/iStockphoto; 29, © SL_Photography/iStockphoto,
© SolStock/iStockphoto, © TT/iStockphoto, © aedkais/iStockphoto, and © South_
agency/iStockphoto.

President: Jen Jenson
Director of Product Development: Spencer Brinker
Senior Editor: Allison Juda
Associate Editor: Charly Haley
Senior Designer: Colin O'Dea

Library of Congress Cataloging-in-Publication Data

Names: Bergin, Raymond, 1968- author.
Title: Animals in danger / by Raymond Bergin.
Description: Minneapolis, Minnesota : Bearport Publishing Company, [2022] |
    Series: What on earth? climate change explained | Includes
    bibliographical references and index.
Identifiers: LCCN 2021039166 (print) | LCCN 2021039167 (ebook) | ISBN
    9781636915555 (library binding) | ISBN 9781636915623 (paperback) | ISBN
    9781636915692 (ebook)
Subjects: LCSH: Wildlife conservation--Juvenile literature. |
    Animals--Climatic factors--Juvenile literature. | Endangered
    species--Juvenile literature. | Climatic changes--Juvenile literature.
Classification: LCC QH75 .B475 2022 (print) | LCC QH75 (ebook) | DDC
    333.95/416--dc23
LC record available at https://lccn.loc.gov/2021039166
LC ebook record available at https://lccn.loc.gov/2021039167

For more information, write to Bearport Publishing, 5357 Penn Avenue South, Minneapolis,
MN 55419. Printed in the United States of America.

Contents

An Overheating Home

A small, furry, mouselike mammal is hot and thirsty. Its mountain home has gotten a lot warmer over the last few years.

This overheated creature is the American pika. It's used to temperatures below freezing. The small animal can't survive if it's too hot. If temperatures reach even 78 degrees Fahrenheit (26 degrees Celsius), it can die. As mountain temperatures have risen, the pika has moved higher in order to escape the heat. But now it lives at the top of the mountain and doesn't have anywhere higher to go. And the heat keeps increasing.

The American pika could soon become one of the first mammals to go **extinct** because of climate change. Its Asian and European cousins are also threatened by rising temperatures.

Heating Up

Our planet is heating up. The warming is caused by human activity, including the use of gas, oil, and coal to power our homes, cars, and devices. Burning these **fossil fuels** releases **carbon dioxide** and other harmful gases into the air. The gases trap heat around the planet, causing the temperatures to rise.

Gases around Earth that trap in heat are called greenhouse gases.

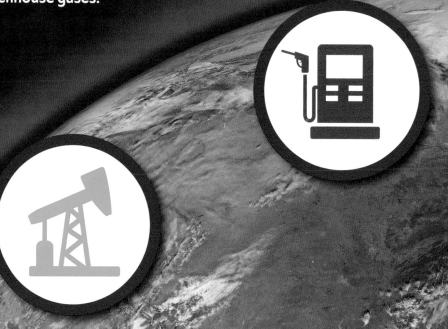

The heat is also changing the climate—or typical weather—around the world. As the climate changes, some animals' homes are changing so much that the creatures can no longer find food, water, or shelter.

As many as a million **species** may be at risk of extinction due to human activity. Climate change may kill off one-third of all living plant and animal species by 2070.

A Melting Home

While the entire planet is warming, the Arctic—the cold, icy area around the North Pole—is heating up twice as fast as the rest of the world. The sea ice there, which many animals need for survival, is melting.

Polar bears in the Arctic hunt for seals on floating sheets of ice. They often have to swim between chunks of sea ice. As Arctic ice melts, polar bears are finding fewer seals and must swim longer distances between pieces of ice. They are becoming so hungry and exhausted that they are in danger of extinction by 2100.

Seals are suffering because of the melting ice, too. The fish they catch at the ice's edge are disappearing with the ice.

If sea ice is spread too far apart, polar bears can't get the rest they need and they may drown.

Coral in Crisis

Melting ice isn't the only danger out at sea. About a third of the carbon dioxide we create by burning fossil fuels ends up in the ocean. This makes the seawater more **acidic**. Some plants and animals, including coral reefs, can't live in water that becomes too acidic.

Warmer, more acidic ocean waters are killing the **algae** that live inside coral and help feed and strengthen coral reefs. Without enough algae, corals become weak and die. Then, the fish and other sea creatures that create homes, raise their young, and find food in the reefs are at risk, too.

When corals are stressed, they might turn white. This is called coral bleaching.

About 25 percent of the ocean's fish depend on healthy coral reefs for their survival. A single area of reefs in Hawaii supports more than 7,000 species of plants and animals.

Danger along the Coast

Closer to shore, warmer waters are making life more difficult for coastal creatures, too. When water warms up, it expands, or takes up more space. As ocean temperatures rise, seawater spreads out and pushes farther onshore. In some coastal areas, this causes flooding, especially at **high tides** or during strong ocean storms. In the United States, more than 200 plant and animal species are **endangered** because of rising sea levels.

Flooding sometimes carries the nests of endangered loggerhead sea turtles right off their beaches. Higher air temperatures can also make the beach sand too hot for the turtle eggs.

Dying of Thirst

Flooding is destroying the homes of coastal animals. But as global temperatures rise, other animals are struggling to find *enough* water. Worldwide, dry places are getting drier because hotter air is drawing more moisture from the earth. This leads to less rainfall, which means rivers, lakes, and ponds dry up even faster. With low water levels, fish are dying, and other animals are forced to wander far from home to find water to drink.

African elephants drink up to 80 gallons (300 L) of water every day! In 2019, more than 200 elephants died during a **drought** in the African country Zimbabwe.

There's Nothing to Eat!

Dry weather can also make it hard for animals to find enough food. Every year, monarch butterflies **migrate** long distances to warmer lands for the winter. Monarch butterflies lay eggs on milkweed plants, which are the only food their caterpillars eat. But many of the areas the butterflies travel through are so dry that milkweed has disappeared.

Without this plant, the number of monarchs that spent the winter in Mexico decreased 80 percent in the last 20 years. Millions of monarchs also used to winter in California, but fewer than 2,000 were counted in 2020.

The milkweed that does manage to grow is absorbing more harmful carbon dioxide. When milkweed absorbs too much of this gas, it creates a poison that harms caterpillars.

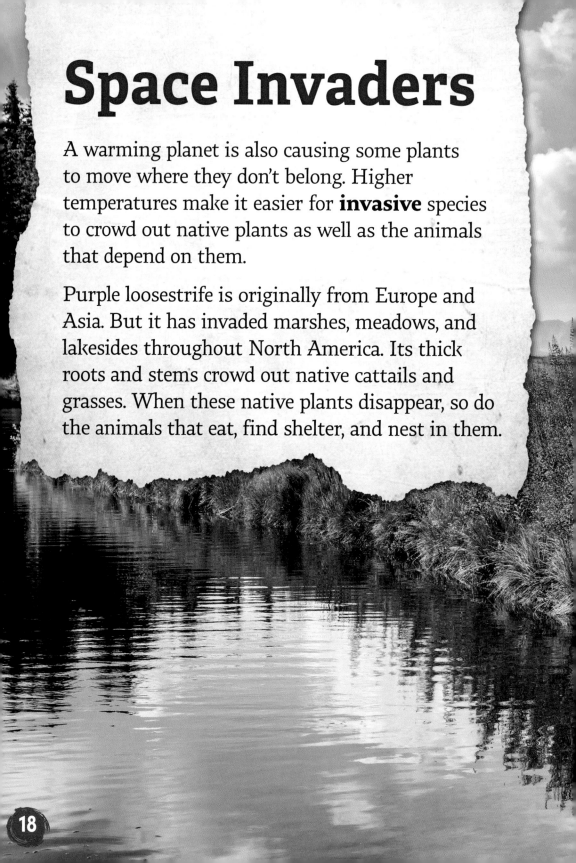

Space Invaders

A warming planet is also causing some plants to move where they don't belong. Higher temperatures make it easier for **invasive** species to crowd out native plants as well as the animals that depend on them.

Purple loosestrife is originally from Europe and Asia. But it has invaded marshes, meadows, and lakesides throughout North America. Its thick roots and stems crowd out native cattails and grasses. When these native plants disappear, so do the animals that eat, find shelter, and nest in them.

Purple loosestrife takes over an area quickly by releasing millions of seeds. The changing climate is allowing loosestrife seeds to bloom earlier, giving the plants more time to grow and spread even more seeds.

Animals on the Move

Today, many animals are leaving their usual homes to find food and shelter elsewhere. This is affecting animals in different ways. While a changing climate is shrinking the **territories** of some, warmer temperatures are letting other animals roam in even larger spaces.

Starving Arctic polar bears are heading onto land, looking for food to replace the seals that are disappearing with the sea ice. On land, they are finding grizzly bears. A warmer, less icy Arctic offers grizzlies more food options for longer periods of the year. These two kinds of bears now fight for control over the same territory.

Today, half of all Earth's species are shifting their ranges. Land animals are moving 10 miles (16 km) per decade. Ocean animals are moving four times faster.

Grizzlies are now spending more time in the warmer, less icy Arctic.

Trapped!

Climate change has many animals on the move. But what about animals who can't move to safety quickly?

Australia's koalas have faced **habitat** loss for years at the hands of humans. Then, in 2019 and 2020, parts of Australia faced a severe drought made worse by climate change. Powerful wildfires broke out. But because so much of the koalas' habitat had already been destroyed, they had nowhere to escape to when the fires raged.

Australia's 2019 and 2020 wildfires killed as many as 10,000 koalas. In total, that means we lost about one-third of Australia's koala population.

What Season Is It?

Some animals, such as the monarch, have always been on the move. They travel with the seasons. As the planet heats up, however, winters become shorter and warmer, and this is disrupting the natural cycle for many migrating animals.

The European pied flycatcher winters in Africa. When the days get longer in spring, it flies to Europe to lay eggs. Once hatched, the baby birds feed on caterpillars found on young oak leaves. But with shorter, milder winters, the oak leaves are popping out earlier. By the time hungry flycatcher babies hatch, the caterpillars have already grown into moths.

Greenland caribou face a similar problem. In spring, caribou move inland to eat Arctic plants. But these plants grow earlier than they used to. They're less **nutritious** by the time caribou arrive. Fewer caribou calves survive each year due to the changing diet.

A European
pied flycatcher

What Are We Doing about It?

The threat to animals due to climate change is real. But all over the world, people are working hard to protect these animals. Some people have **preserved** and **restored** natural lands. Others are cleaning pollution from the oceans. The countries and peoples of the Arctic are carefully protecting the remaining ice in the area. Engineers and scientists are also developing energy that takes power from the sun, wind, and water without polluting the planet.

If we work together to protect the planet, the future will be bright for all animals—and for us!

Florida created a protected chain of forests, swamps, fields, rivers, and streams. This land allows 131 threatened animal species to move freely in search of food, water, and shelter.

Save Animals in Danger!

The problems animals are facing are a sign that the planet is unhealthy. You can help animals by keeping their habitats clean and safe. What can you do to save animals in danger?

Visit a national wildlife refuge or park. Supporting these lands helps to protect and provide homes for endangered animals and plants.

Volunteer at a local nature center. Learn about endangered animals in your area and teach your friends and family how to protect them.

Turn your backyard or community garden into a wildlife habitat. Put up bird feeders. Plant native plants and trees to provide homes and food for wildlife.

Avoid using harmful chemicals to control weeds and pests on your lawn or garden. These chemicals can make animals sick and poison the soil.

Join—or plan your own—community cleanup days to keep natural areas clear of garbage.

Glossary

acidic containing a chemical that has a very sharp or sour taste

algae tiny plantlike living things often found in bodies of water

carbon dioxide a gas given off when fossil fuels are burned

drought a long period of time with dry weather

endangered in danger of dying out completely

extinct no longer alive; having died out completely

fossil fuels fuels such as coal, oil, and gas made from the remains of plants and other organisms that died millions of years ago

habitat the place in nature where a plant or animal normally lives

high tides the times when seawaters are at their highest levels and come farthest up on land

invasive plants or animals that have been moved from their habitat into another habitat in which they do not naturally belong

migrate to move from one place to another at a certain time of the year

nutritious having things that an animal or person needs to be healthy

preserved kept safe from harm or loss

restored repaired, cleaned, or returned to its original condition

species groups that animals and plants are divided into, according to similar characteristics

territories areas of land that belong to animals and their families

Read More

Cooke, Tim. *A Chemical Nightmare: Bald Eagle Comeback (Saving Animals from the Brink).* Minneapolis: Bearport Publishing, 2022.

Free, Katie. *Animals in Danger: Understanding Climate Change (A True Book: Understanding Climate Change).* New York: Children's Press, 2020.

Jenkins, Martin. *Under Threat: An Album of Endangered Animals.* Somerville, MA: Candlewick Press, 2019.

Minoglio, Andrea. *Our World Out of Balance: Understanding Climate Change and What We Can Do.* San Francisco: Blue Dot Kids Press, 2021.

Learn More Online

1. Go to **www.factsurfer.com** or scan the QR code below.

2. Enter "**Animals in Danger**" into the search box.

3. Click on the cover of this book to see a list of websites.

Index

About the Author

Raymond Bergin is a writer living in New Jersey. He has put up dozens of bird houses and feeders throughout his property to help support the stressed and threatened bird populations in his area. This summer, he was thrilled to see several monarch butterflies feeding on his milkweed plants.